The Winds of Home Have Names

poems by

Diana Elser

Finishing Line Press
Georgetown, Kentucky

The Winds of Home Have Names

for Dad

Copyright © 2021 by Diana Elser
ISBN 000-0-00000-000-0   First Edition
All rights reserved under International and Pan-American Copyright Conventions. No part of this book may be reproduced in any manner whatsoever without written permission from the publisher, except in the case of brief quotations embodied in critical articles and reviews.

ACKNOWLEDGMENTS

Thank you Hugo House in Seattle for wonderful classes, instructors and students who keep me inspired and writing, in particular Deborah Woodard, poet, generous mentor, and creator of extraordinary prompts. Thanks to the Jackson Hole Writers Conference where Laurie Kutchins, resident faculty and poet (Associate Professor of English at James Madison University, Virginia), offered her steady 'hand at my back' from the beginning. Elizabeth Cohen, poet, writer, editor (Associate Professor of creative writing at SUNY, Plattsburgh) was skilled and merciless in the best way. Finally, thanks to M. J. McDermott who I met in a class at Hugo House. She's the meteorologist for Q13 Fox in Tacoma and reviewed the science in the poems to assure accuracy.

Publisher: Leah Huete de Maines
Editor: Christen Kincaid
Cover Art: Derek Schleich using personal and family photos
Author Photo: Chris Schleich
Cover Design: Elizabeth Maines McCleavy

Printed in the USA on acid-free paper.
Order online: www.finishinglinepress.com
      also available on amazon.com

Author inquiries and mail orders:
Finishing Line Press
P. O. Box 1626
Georgetown, Kentucky 40324
U. S. A.

Table of Contents

Memory Buckled for Takeoff 1

Radiosonde 2

Driving the Interstate Corridor 3

Climate Change 4

Haboob in Black and White, El Paso – 1956 5

What My Father Built 6

I Do and Other Probabilities 7

"With Precision of a Wizard…" 8

Routine Seasonal Variation 9

Calculating Possibilities 10

Hard Weather, Dimming Hearts 11

Poor Visibility 14

Small Town Drought 15

Thirsty Again 16

High Wind Warning 17

In Lieu of Rain 19

Navigating Blind 20

Out of Season 21

Rest Stops Attract Ghouls Who Find the Plumbing Irresistible .. 22

Remaindered, 1979 23

Joseph's Fishing Resort 24

Glacier Point, Yosemite Valley 26

Relief 27

Memory Buckled for Takeoff

Exceptional weather, wind chill a factor
under moon ringed with icy curve,
a footstep into snowstorm stories
in which you earn your way, learn your lines,
pluck a broken ukulele – spelunk
        in the family boneyard

where you trip on a rotting femur,
a cracked skull kissing its own jawbone,
vertebrae scattered like insect husks,
like bots sorting prophecies delivered
by computer-model magicians
        simulating, spinning the circular unexpected.

Debacles of human weather
rage and buckle –
crush of ranunculus, crash of big data
spice a peculiar treacle, parts ridicule,
        heresy, insoluble toxin.

Deep sea diver, trickster-conniver
I practice ventricular acrobatics
under a cloudbank of exhalation.
Cable taut, the funicular grabs, see me?
        Tucked in and hunkered, showing you

I can take it, I can do it,
tools in hand, knuckled down to polish
        a carbuncle of gratitude.

Radiosonde

My father drives into a snowstorm
big in his winter hat, coat, gloves.
Windshield wipers thump, dry heat blows
soft, the snow tires make a funny sound.
We float in snow, night poked open by headlights.
A deer, Dad says, when we see shiny eyes.

He slows the car, turns onto a short road with a gate
leaves the motor on so I'll be warm,
tells me to watch out the window.
The car door thunks – I get to my knees on the seat
wipe a clear spot on the steamed window.

Snowflakes make him blurry, his boots make a ditch.
He opens a gate, goes into a little house,
comes out holding the biggest balloon I have ever seen,
all white, lifts his arms and the balloon bumps into the snowflakes,
up and up into the dark until I can't see it.

When he's back in the car
I want to know where the balloons go –
he says *higher than you have ever been and
higher than I have ever been.*
I ask why. He tells me how *pilots need to know
the weather before they fly.*

I tell him I want to see the balloon go up again.
He says they go up every night, every day, everywhere.
Now we're driving, and I want to know
how big is the sky. *Pretty big*, he says, *the higher
the balloons go, the colder it is.* I'm sleepy
with questions I have no words for,
eyelids heavy with balloons.

Note: A radiosonde is a battery-powered telemetry instrument package carried by a weather balloon into the atmosphere to measure various atmospheric parameters and transmit them by radio to a ground receiver. Weather balloons are launched simultaneously twice a day from weather stations around the world.

Driving the Interstate Corridor

Cloud-borne, at work on Olympus in the temples
of the Greek mythology he loved – my father,
meteorologist to the Gods, bent over maps, conjuring jet streams,
ocean currents, monsoon and drought –
playing politics with Zeus, Poseidon, Apollo, the Anemoi wind brothers,
watching their strut-and-rut concoctions – vengeful gales,
lightning bolts and floods – despising their cruelty to humans.

On earth, he found his place and took it,
like someone does who grew up in the weather of distinct seasons,
tending animals, crops, irrigation ditches.
Schooled in weather's math and paths, the limits
and wonder of prediction,
the forecast that told his end went uncharted
like our isobaric wail and keen.

Today, the West he loved lays everything before me.
I need no map for this ritual road between homes:
I-15 north out of Salt Lake City and Ogden,
I-84 northwest through Burley, Twin Falls, Mountain Home, Boise.
One hundred degree-ground temps bend the air.
Pale cirri flick across a scrubbed sky, spring wheat stands ripe,
first hay crops lie mown, ready to bale.

The Ogden, Weber, Snake and Payette rivers
run high for July. Traffic's light, shoulder stripe glares
in the side-view mirror. Sunscreen gloves on my hands
burn white in the windshield reflection.
Broken center lane lines repeat.
Here's the airport and fire-weather center
where he worked, the hospital where he died,
then Meridian, where he and mom lived last.

Cool air blows over my bare arms.
I ignore the Sirens' time-broken call
telling me I can still go back –
tucked under the driver's seat,
his boxed and sealed ashes.

Climate Change

In Idaho after Christmas
thin whiskered cheek against my smooth one,
my father's last words, *drive safe*
my frozen throat, we left

sooner than I wanted, too soon
returned to mid-January's hard freeze,
my living belly swathed in soft black hose,
black slip, black dress, baby curled, quiet.

Sticks for trees, no birds,
high black boots on icy sidewalks
strewn with fireplace ash and salt
to keep us upright, keep us from falling
ashes everywhere, falling snow.

March in southern California, the best day
of that pregnancy, I talked with a friend,
fell asleep late –
in the morning on the patio ate croissants
with butter, the baby heavy, kicking.

I wore white flannel and lace, my eight-month belly
rose out of the white wrought-iron lounge
as did my neck out of lace ruffle,
bathed in sun, maple, oak, eucalyptus
leaking birdsong.

Haboob in Black and White, El Paso – 1956

Old box camera slung around his neck,
Dad must have hopped the rock wall
as the storm front bulged over the Franklin Mountains,
pulled himself onto the roof of our house
bent on capturing the brown curved wall,
part cloud, part dust
looming closer in each exposure,
big and dark enough in the last shots to dim the sun –
a spring haboob plowing across the Chihuahua Desert,
pictures and data published months later
in the *Bulletin of the American Meteorological Society.*

We hated the dust storms for the itch and sting, our gummy eyes.
They erased our desert forts, sand-scoured our legs.
Grit in our teeth and noses, we waited them out inside,
drew pictures with our fingers on coated venetian blinds
suspended over window sills with little dunes
silted in the corners.

Every Wednesday in third grade,
each of us received the *Weekly Reader,*
mini-versions of our parents' newspapers,
different color borders each week,
orange the week his two photos appeared
with an article on dust storms,
his name in tiny print underneath the snapshots –
ink-smeared by my finger into scrapbook daydream
how my name could be in the *Weekly Reader*
my face on the cover of *Time* and I knew
I would get to ride in a rocket ship.

What My Father Built

I watched my father measure, draw pictures on graph paper
with a T square, label with numbers the feet and inches.
Went with him to the lumberyard, watched him measure again at home

covered my ears from the circular saw's whine,
held pieces of wood in place against the handsaw, hacksaw
zzzz and *shsh*, the hammer *wham*.

Wood chisel, level, plane, sander, Phillips, flathead,
sometimes I got to help drill holes, twist screws, hit nails,
mount handles, knobs, hinges.

For the sixth grade science fair
I chose to build an anemometer with wood scraps from the garage –
a plywood square marked with an arc:

wind speed in miles per hour, a smaller plywood rectangle
attached to a wooden stick to make a paddle that would
catch the wind.

I trimmed the five-eighths boards, picked off splinters,
sanded edges, nailed the paddle to its handle,
bolted it to the bigger board, painted everything white,

the paddle black, made up a scale – paddle straight down
at zero, hypothesis: wind speed equal to where on the numbered arc
the wind blew the paddle –

so clear to the straight-A student, underexposed to failure,
to the rudiments of instrumentation, calibration standards,
who didn't think she needed help, like a teacher's

or a father's tactful suggestion: *let's look at a real anemometer*,
those tiny, finely lubricated weightless cups
I had seen spinning at the airport tower.

Finely calibrated, attuned to adult reactions –
Dad's face, a funny look, less enthusiasm than I expected
as pride in me collided with his moral conviction
that in this instance, I be left to my own devices.

I Do and Other Probabilities

When the skies lowered over the Bear Tooth Mountains
at my second cousin's wedding, it was sunny –
afternoon showers likely but clearing –
my father's weather forecast words.

Afternoon wind brought rain-spatter, colder air,
drove us into the tent. We moved our chairs onto the tent flaps
at the raised floor's edge, and sat,
so the storm could not strip away our cover.

Thunder-lightning-hail threw themselves
around the valley – sleet fell like rice then rain,
quiet air, a clearing sky, twilight,
we ate and talked for hours.

I knew exactly where he would sit, who
he would dance with first, what he would drink
if he were still here in the mountain weather
and the extended family he knew by heart.

The unsuspecting younger ones line up for a piece of wedding cake
their lives forecast with imaginary certainty
like the bride's dress they sewed her into –
a minute-by-minute stay-tuned storm prediction of perfect fit,

confection tossed on a blanket, seductive
as her hailed-on shoulders and frontal cumuli-bosom.
Haptic accident that the hailstones felt like tulle.
Our hectic stomp did not bring down the tent,
or spare us from the altitude.

"With Precision of a Wizard…"
—for Isaac Cline, early meteorologist b 1852 – d 1955

is what the award said, because
Isaac Cline predicted the 1927
Mississippi Flood two weeks in advance
so only 254 died across seven states
covered in water ten to thirty feet deep,
six hundred thousand homeless –

disaster forgotten unless you were there.

He never stopped
remembering that success.
Never stopped remembering
thirty years earlier, his failure to predict,
post warnings, when his *absurd delusion*
materialized, a severe tropical storm
rolling over the Gulf of Mexico into Galveston,

elevation 8.7 feet.

Family and dozens of neighbors huddled
in his house on stilts three blocks from the beach,
where his certain science did not hold
against *impossible* 140 mile-an-hour winds
driving the rain, the storm surge
that crossed the shallow sandy bar
to take the town of thousands,
his house, his pregnant wife.

Three daughters survived, and he revised his science.

Every year an award in his name
goes to someone for wizarding their best –
a prize, because the story became
that he did warn Galveston,
when the real story was something else –

forgotten, unless you were there.

Routine Seasonal Variation

Minute-by-minute Dad died before his time,
his weather forecasting skills
focused on satellite imagery, jet stream anomalies,
lightning strike frequencies, the stuff of briefings

for newspapers, broadcasts, pilots, farmers and fire fighters –
routine seasonal variations layered
over office politics, paperwork,
grass demanding a mower –

not on the hints his body presented –
below average chill, more tired more often, odd accidents,
less chance of, and less, comfort.
Data pointed to no more than age,

not to the invisible cellular storm
percolating in the gut, the colon,
wearing away a shoreline where climate and weather
beat at bedrock.

With a full calendar, the facts, happiness
wedded to ignorance
we smile gamely at the forecast
which looks nothing like the black hood
that prevents us from seeing the axe.

Calculating Possibilities

If all the weather happened all at once
imagine piled upon the bed, tangled hangars –
you dress inside then run back out
putting up your hood
to save your head from wet, from cold,
from hail or snow
waxy balm to soothe chapped lips
sunglasses or goggles to fight the glare, you paw
through socks and special under layers

and sun is not your friend though you crave the light,
you must have a hat to shade ears, neck and face
sunscreen for all of those,
and appendages
loose clothes in lightweight fabrics to let air circulate,
wick the sweat away
same as your cold-weather gear must wick the sweat
while keeping out the chill

You layer up and peel off fleeciness and bulk –
Mackinaws and parkas, anoraks and slickers
Wellingtons and mukluks,
Tevas, and Sorels
mittens, mufflers, gloves and muffs
chullos and sou'westers,
tuques and balaclavas, dickies and bandannas –
ice cleats, boots, water-snow-or rock shoes
drysuits, wetsuits, shortie or full
Thinsulate, Smartwool, Sun Shield and Spandex
Sunbrella, Neoprene, Lycra, and Goretex,
short-sleeved, long-sleeved,
hooded or slip-on,
anti-bacterial and odor-reducing,
sunproof, windproof, waterproof or resistant –

clothing protection, an endless selection
while the weather comes to you naked

Hard Weather, Dimming Hearts

I
Skilled at exploratory voyages that plant a flag, make a claim
we watch the camellias out front bloom
four months early, lilacs burst purple not in spring, but fall.

Pumpkins bloom to exhaustion, never set, while we huddle,
refusing to admit, forget or forgive one another.

Inconceivable: that the earth would give in to us,
become something different than what it was when we began,
changing as it always has, this time using code we fed it,
code we did not understand we wrote, as our numbers grew:

what we killed and ate, what we bought and sold, burned and threw away.

II
Today, the weather keeps me here, at home,
so I couldn't tell you about my storm of discontent, dancing
as I am on broken polar ice that reflects sun's heat,
insulates the polar seas.

I'm willing to risk this thinning ice, but I can't dance
on dark and open waters, so dance loose and fast where I can,
hoping for the best.

Instructions: Warmer atmosphere holds more moisture,
warming sea surface under warmer air increases my thirst
until the rains-that-seldom-stop, start, and the ice is gone.
I ride the water cycle faster, spinning a spiraled call-out
to Revelation's seven angels, seven trumpets blaring,

their giant white wings beat the tropopause.

III
We're angel stricken, ocean-lapped, rain-soaked,
lightning-struck, dying of thirst
on the long march to Sanctuary.   Haven.   Asylum.
Water, food and restitution, but oh the loneliness,
the heat, the cold, the losses drive us mad.

Wind, sun, grief rotate the fan that moves the air to cool us
so we have the strength to swat the flies that dog us
like the greedy hormones that drive us to desire.

Invisible: bad cholesterol and plaque cling to vessel walls,
break loose into our tiny bloody rivers.
We cough gobs of dirty spit, adjust our feckless masks,
the air becomes the enemy.

Bodies built to save us turn against us, sabotaged.

These changes – libido or albedo – don't automatically mean
we love earth less, something else more,
or that the long summer of first love, that sexy Holocene moment
will, or would, or could last forever.

Impossible: that like the earth turning away from us,
we could grow to hate one another, or become indifferent,
that earth itself could say *enough*.

IV
What stays at home unloved becomes predictable weather.
We'll do anything to hold ourselves in place –
create more confusion, more wars, more extreme events,
more eye-of-the-storm silences that make the math,

the odds that such events will occur more often
add up to *meaningful trends over time* that we choose to disbelieve
until the seventh angel's vial of wrath pours out destruction –
thunder, lightning, earthquake, hail, famine, flood –

everyone and everything you love at risk,
disrupted food supplies, colony collapse,
bids and battles for water harangue the poisoned air,
compassion strangles.

Incantation: Lord where is thy refuge, my people, my planet –
we could have seen, we did see, the winds begin to spin the clouds,
the weather was not beyond us.

V
Natural order ill-defined, human-defined disaster
laid out on wet and molded carpets piled with sodden insulation.
Extinctions, migrations rot under paper storms:
visas, insurance claims, proof of citizenship,
property rights, suits and countersuits,
mountains of a thing called plastic – acres of tents,
fire-blasted houses in blackened forests.

High tides of fishless waters climb and stay, homes sag, and sink.

We had to be poor, come from nothing before we could be driven
by every desire, before purchase and sale could drive our desires deeper,
blow them high. We never meant to love money more.
But that was then, and here we are,

Inarguably: a crowd of billions counting icicles
in a non-existent court, abandoned and displaced,
buying our monthly allotments of drinking water,
lined up for bread, counting the dead.

Poor Visibility

It might be 1983 before the anesthesia wore off –

or 1962 walking to school through
the mist-draped neighborhood

or 1954's glued-on cotton clouds stuck to my first-grade
picture of home.

This fog's gray-gloved fingers parse the islands in the Sound
feel their way

badgered by temperature and grief's cold weight
to commit and confess foggish sins of deception –

deny visibility   cancel color   suffocate sound

fool everyone who wants to forget,
wants to move too fast.

Small Town Drought

Having gathered what's allowed by scant winter snowfall
the river-fed Great Salt Lake takes its only exit from the basin
and evaporates, too salty for fish at the southern end,
dense with microscopic brine shrimp, sand flies –
a bird-haven.

Fifth year in a row, the town on the edge of the salt flats
begs rain. Wilted gardens dry early to yellow, brown.
Heat-strangled, shiny browed, irritated
with the squint-eyed sky, bare feet pavement-burned –

we drive to the glittering waterline, the lake
where we become mythical salt-buoyed fish,
paddling crooked circles, chasing the floating beer cooler,
flopped on our backs on our blow-up mats like sick pets
belly-up in a home aquarium.

Scalp and skin-prickled with sun-blasted salt rime,
we head for the blue-tarp shade, thirsty, a little drunk,
douse one another with bottled water, call it our rain-dance
while we suck on mushy lime and cherry popsicles.

We raise a cold-water toast to the sky-water mirage,
talk about the shrunken inland sea, rain-makers, cloud-seeding –
how we'd like to hike the Uinta Mountains sixty miles east,
stick bare feet into snowmelt creeks running icy-high –
edged with green, chilly-wet.

Thirsty Again

Agonal gusts
        whip, scrawl themselves
                on a weather tarp's flapping
                      blat and snap,

        crack and drop an old cottonwood's
                          upper trunk.

Sudden-rain cold, we're caught by instant wet,
        faces slick with big drops,
                cloud-grumbles close in –
                            light sprints past sound

glimmer-flash-upset, quick-glare strobes the landscape,
        sends us inside
                slipping, ear-slapped, soaked.

Dripping, we towel off
        in a metal drum beaten with sticks, we're deaf,
                rain-thrashed
                          wind-shrieked,
water gushes beyond gutters,
        dark rushes the windows
                            door slams open
we crowd against what would still take us,
        slide down to hold, and hold.

In new quiet, temperature up, we twitch,
        humidity ticks the air, pressure up,
                sunlight bends through the west rain-licked window.

Wet clothes stripped away, we rest.

Next morning, you'd never know except the cistern's full,
        landscape crisp as clean laundry,
                a fresh gravel fan like a brushstroke
                        at the bottom of the wash.

By afternoon, heat-cracked mud – skies blue with dry.

High Wind Warning
> Inspired by a 1982 Oakland Tribune newspaper clipping,
> They Call the Wind Cockeyed Bob.

Humans name the winds of home
like they name their children, their pets,
familiar as the home horizon, color of the soil, taste of local water:

Afghanistan's *wind of 120 days*, the Central American *chubasco*,
dry and hot *khamsin* of the Middle East, *suhaili* over the Persian Gulf,
elephanta of southwestern India; *steppenwind* in Russia,
North African *sirocco*, Alaskan *taku*, Siberia's *viuga*,
North American high plains' *Alberta clipper*,
the *mistral* of Provence – *waimea, matsukaze, williwaw, imba, rok* –

I find the clipping thirty-five years after Dad's death,
a wind-sampler that triggers a brain-locked dust-devil,
makes me long to call or write.

I would talk first about the *chinook*, mid-winter surprise
when we lived in Montana, the mysterious name, sudden warmth
that melted snow cover, left us slogging home from school in mud,
coats off, earth and vegetation smells spelling spring.

I'd say his first grandchild, *Jamie*, the one he knew,
lives on the Carquinez Straits inland from San Francisco Bay toward the Delta,
where the seasonal *diablo* blows hot and dry,
high pressure in Nevada pushing warm air over the Sierras.

I'd mention *Derek* whom he never met, the youngest grandson,
living in Seattle where to the north the *squamish*
whirls up violent in the fjords, dissipates at sea, while to the south
the *gorge wind*, the *coho* drives whitecaps on the Columbia.

I'd tell him that in southern California, a sister-wind to the *diablo*,
the *Santa Ana*, also born of Nevada heat,
swells above the San Gabriels,
rushes to the Pacific where his oldest grandson, *Christopher*, lives –
born three months after he died, father to his twin great-granddaughters –

But I am done with this one-sided conversation, cannot say
any more names for small talk with a ghost, no matter how beloved.

Nostalgia, the universal breeze of lost attachments
spins to *wind-shear* – knocks me sideways.

In Lieu of Rain
> *-all the water on earth is all the water there ever was, and ever will be*

If all the words on earth were water, ninety-seven percent
would be salty conversation moving in thermal layers,
cold words sinking hotter words rising,

> water and words in warm and cold currents

pulled by moon and earth's rotations, tidal words
crawling onto beaches and off, where those who speak
walk with nets, dig wells, build rain-catcher wordtraps.

Only three percent of words-as-water would be fresh –
seventy-five percent of that locked in glaciers and ice sheets,
words calving in chunks, melting.

Twenty-four percent would pool in dark aquifers and moistened soils
where water leaks into caverns, drips off stalactites, layers itself
into wordy stalagmites scaling into echo.

Zero point three-three percent would flow to fresh-water rivers and lakes
used more often in far more than 0.33% of all dark and cold
conversations – the infinitesimal remainder lost to faulty memory,
released by plants in silent transpiration.

> Word-chatter precipitates: rain, snow, hail and dew, all

float and fall, fill the rising ocean pages. Word-drops ripple,
condense, clouds of meaning rise from significant tongues,
unable to make rain where dryness reigns, words fail.

Riverbeds run high with dust, words undrinkable,
vocabularies collapsed into aquifers too deep to reach, or empty,
strewn with husks of river nymphs, water gods, sprites,

> the world's living things waiting – wordless, scrambling, thirsty.

Navigating Blind

In slow and regal tones
fog horns on the straits
shape the winter morning

while you, somewhere
in memory's coastal fog
rise to find me

under a clear inland sky
the measured chant
calls to me, here

where the children wake up
cheerful and the furnace
blows dry air

flavored
with coffee and toast.
I'm afloat

in week-end messes,
Monday chores,
shoreline detritus,

years away from
when you pointed
to places on a map.

Fog horns
deny
the morning sun,

my hand
brushed your shoulder,
your hand

came and went
in grief and want
like morning fog.

Out of Season

I could swear it's autumn in this mountain valley,
pale sun, milky light, clearing sky that doesn't clear.
Cold gusts offset warm sun breaks,
air smells like damp earth, pinesap,
someone's fireplace smoke, moldy leaves.

I'm at Mom's house, but summer comes next, not winter.
These are last year's leaves my brother Ray never got to.

In the backyard on my knees under budding aspen
covered in leaf crumbles and dead grass,
I gather one pile at a time, sneeze,
stuff another black plastic garbage bag,
tie it off, carry a few at a time to the front –
all of this so familiar my father will walk around the corner
in his plaid wool, take a glove off to blow his nose,
say something funny about working-smart-not-hard –

but I am here to bag leaves for my brother
who lives with my mother, tends
to her shrinking, her growing pile of confusions
as she talks to me about her husband, my father,
as if I did not know him – *he was nice, you would have liked him,
everyone did.* I say *weren't you the lucky one?*
She nods, pleased with the love invoked,
pleased again when she finds the garden gloves I ask for.
She asks again *now what is it you're doing?*

Pulling the gloves snug as the sorrow she elicits,
I tell her, again – *I'm bagging leaves to help Ray*
and I don't say – so he, my brother, the boy, your son,
my father, your husband, that nice man –
won't have to do it after work.

She nods, says *he's gone a lot, but he always comes back.*

Rest Stops Attract Ghouls Who Find the Plumbing Irresistible

Washington rest stop, just across the Columbia,
Gee Creek – where ghouls are said to gather –
outside the restroom, press a button by the water fountains
labeled underneath white letters on blue
PUSH BUTTON FOR WEATHER FORECAST.
An embedded speaker spills out
Portland-Seattle information – coastal, inland,
a link to the NOAA frequency.
I speak into it saying, *Dad I think about you.*
A man passing says *You know that's not a microphone?*
and I'm sure I hear a ghoul snicker.
I know, I know, but it could be I mumble,
when I want to say "Who the hell asked you?
and how do you know he can't hear me?"
The water fountains come on, no one bent to drink –
it's the ghouls I'm sure, they love the water
transparent like themselves, and fluid.
They care nothing for the weather.

Remaindered, 1979

I find the tie clasp in its plastic box
stored in the dresser-top tray
with his Freemason's ring,
a few small tie tacks,
the bolos he eventually preferred to neckties,
his watch, military pins and ribbons.
I lay one hand over all of it, looking for magic.
                Nothing.

In Thailand, 1971, because everything was cheap
we bought souvenirs for everyone.
I designed a tie clip to honor
my father's weather profession.
Using my sketch, the artist etched in silver
raindrop and snowflake, cumulus cloud slashed
by lightning flash, sun shining behind.

But the weld of heavy clip to cloud and sun
added weight, pulled at itself throughout the day
until it hung crooked.
On a fat tie, it angled down slowly.
On a thinner tie it dropped off altogether,
and eight years later he was dead.

                I lift the box, take off the lid.

Tarnished, the clip lies heavy in my palm.
I touch the lightning bolt's sharp tip,
slip the clip onto my lapel. It tilts,
true to design and memory, begins to slide.

Joseph's Fishing Resort

Nine-thirty AM, *Ahab the A-rab* on the juke box,
pool balls clicking in this San Pablo Bay café and bar
hung over the water on wooden planks nailed
across wooden piers sunk in mud, not a visible
right angle inside or out. I can see and hear lapping water
through the floor. Always makes me smile –
I don't belong here.

But of course I do, because anyone who shows up
and sticks to a few rules belongs – that's the kind of place
it's meant to be. I see the familiar others,
we nod, don't say much, part of the rules.
They don't know me nor I them – just that sometimes
we're here, them more than me so far –
I don't want to belong here,

and I always come back. Several faces hunger
for less last night, less booze, more sleep, is what I guess.
I'm here to mourn, and work, in that order.
Kids in school, dinner planned. You pour your own
coffee refills with a shot if you want, which I do
while the morning fog yawns away to the west.

I don't know Bill, the owner, except he's a rich, gay alcoholic
who owns a lot of property. He makes soup fresh daily,
cream of mushroom my favorite.
I watch him reeling in lost souls, his face marked by pain
and wit, a will to fish, lines always in the water. *This morning,
he says, offering a rare and slight smile as he adds my shot
Port Costa was cold, the sun doesn't get there until later, it's
aways down the Straits. I get up, feed the ducks and geese.*

"– and I'll bet they talk back too," I quip, thinking about
managing drunks in my bartending days. He gives me a look,
unsure what I mean. I don't say more, go back to my book,
I know the rules. The black Labrador pup, new red bandana knotted
at her neck, whines as Bill feeds the fire in the corner stove,
stops when he shushes her.

Soothed is what I am, comforted by this place, where I am
modestly naughty, sucking up whiskey-laced coffee

on a school day, writing again, resurrecting my father
with words: me. All grown up, mom and school-board member,
married, only a little unhappy –
of course I belong here.

Glacier Point, Yosemite Valley

I did not think of you
on purpose, standing on that cliff,
of and with the place, not "in" it.

Maybe it was your hands
lifted something from, and off me,
pulled that stubborn snake's

sussuration, the long hiss – out.
Shutters clicked and clicked
and you were not lost, nor I

and I was not bereft, but left
to be where I was needed,
atomically intimate

you and I woven into air
anatomically incorrect
within apart, and yes

or no, no matter what we do
or don't, no matter where we are –
this place – not us.

Relief

This morning we noticed
yesterday's December storm
took the top off one of the backyard pines
rising above our three-story house –
ten feet lopped – not on the roof,
in the alley, the yard, or next door.

Today's weather spirits blow in hard
again, blast and bend the trees all afternoon,
rake the yard for anything loose,
badger the windows, walls,
flood gutters and downspouts,
demand we stay inside where we belong.

We shrug off barometric uneasiness,
check flashlights, set out candles,
pull the shades like children
pull blankets over their heads.

That night we dress up to attend
a neighbor's party two houses away,
hunker inside before our own door,
shoulders and chins drawn in – bracing –

but outside, foliage drips in air
warmer than this afternoon, and still.
A bare-waned moon offers itself,
pulls our faces off our chests,
invites us, upright, into the evening.

Unable to reliably find north if she cannot see a north-south running mountain range on the horizon, **Diana Elser** was born in Great Falls, Montana (Rockies to the east), grew up in El Paso, Texas (Franklin Mountains to the west), finished high school in Bountiful, Utah (west slope of the Wasatch Front), and earned a degree in English at Utah State (west slope of the Bear River Mountains). Despite coming from Montana ranch families on both sides, she grew up regretfully suburban. She practices poetry via classes offered at Hugo House in Seattle (west of the Cascades, east of the Olympics), the annual Jackson Hole Writers Conference (southeast of the Tetons), and two poetry groups. She is currently at work on more weather and climate poems, a collection in the voice of a blunt, mouthy grandmother, and collected eye-witness accounts of experiences with ghouls, so far mostly imaginary. She has published recently in *The Chrysanthemum 2020 Literary Anthology* (Goldfish Press), *Rise Up Review* (2017), *Clerestory Poetry Journal* (2017, 2016), and *Writing It Right* (2016, Shaggy Dog Press).

www.ingramcontent.com/pod-product-compliance
Lightning Source LLC
LaVergne TN
LVHW041514070426
835507LV00012B/1557